INTERMITTENT
FASTING FOR BEGINNERS

A COMPLETE GUIDE

Authors Page

Dr.G Janki – BDS, DNHE, PGDC in Nutrition from NIN (Hyderabad).

Dr. G Jnaki is Certified Nutritionist from the National Institute of Nutrition, Premier Nutrition Research Institute has been Relentlessly working on researching and spreading awareness about the importance of Food and Nutrition in preventing and treating various medical conditions, working to share knowledge and experience to all age groups in the field of Food & Nutrition.

She views food as the greatest gift nature has bestowed upon man, and has made it her life mission to help people appreciate and consume healthy wholesome foods and lead healthier, fulfilling disease free life.

*PRE
FACE*

*INTERMITTENT FASTING FOR
BEGINNERS –
A COMPLETE GUIDE gives the clear
information about Intermittent Fasting,
and helps you to clarify all doubts on It.*

CONTENTS

ABOUT INTERMITTENT FASTING

INTRODUCTION TO INTERMITTENT FASTING:

-A phenomenon called intermittent fasting is currently one of the world's most popular health and fitness trends.

-Meaning of intermittent occurring at irregular intervals, not continuous or study. Includes a cycle of eating or not eating (fasting in a day).

- Intermittent fasting is an eating pattern where you cycle between periods of eating and fasting. It does not say anything about which foods to eat, but rather when you should eat them. There are several different intermittent fasting methods, all of which split the day or week into eating periods and fasting periods.

WHEN AND HOW INTERMITTENT FASTING BECAME POPULAR

-in year 2002 Chicago done many experiments and started watch how do people get so much benefits from fasting. They started by eating 4 days and 2 days fast and check the benefits and after doing intermittent fasting they checked the benefits. and they found numerous health benefits.

-The farmers not use to eat anything first 2-3 hours of morning schedule they work eat and work and by 6-7 pm they eat their last meal dinner and after that they do not eat anything next day (it means they use to fast for 16 hours and eat for 8 hours), Actually they use to fallow ideal w16/8 window this as their life style and they are so healthy and strong. Now this method of eating and not eating patter is known as intermittent fasting.

WHO MADE THIS INTERMITTENT FASTING POPULAR:

-Dr Jason fung a health expert who made this intermittent fasting popular.

-He explained when we eat in our eating window our insulin level increases and the food which we eat is stored as a form of sugar in the liver. And later convert into liver fat.

-And same happens reverse in fasting window, when we fast the insulin level decreases and in fasting state as we don't get food our body in turn start utilising the stored fat from liver as energy source

Why Fast?

-Humans have actually been fasting for thousands of years.

-Sometimes it was done out of necessity, when there simply wasn't any food available and then fat is produced in the liver. But this cycle gets reversed when we are in fasting. i.e, when we are not eating anything our insulin level decreases and the fat stored in the liver is burnt to give energy.

- If your fasting window is for long period then your body will be on fat burning mode for longer period. Example: 11 am – 7pm is eating window and 7 pm – next day 11 am is fasting window.

-In other instances, it was done for religious reasons. Various religions, including Hinduism, Islam, Christianity and Buddhism, mandate some form of fasting.

-Humans and other animals also often instinctively fast when sick.

-Clearly, there is nothing "unnatural" about fasting, and our bodies are very well equipped to handle extended periods of not eating.

-All sorts of processes in the body change when we don't eat for a while, in order to allow our bodies to thrive during a period of famine. It has to do with hormones, genes and important cellular repair processes.

-When fasted, we get significant reductions in blood sugar and insulin levels, as well as a drastic increase in human growth hormone.

-Many people do intermittent fasting in order to lose weight, as it is a very simple and effective way to restrict calories and burn fat.

-Others do it for the metabolic health benefits, as it can improve various different risk factors and health markers.

-There is also some evidence that intermittent fasting can help you live longer. Studies in rodents show that it can extend lifespan as effectively as calorie restriction.

-Some research also suggests that it can help protect against diseases, including heart disease, type 2 diabetes, cancer, Alzheimer's disease and others.

-Other people simply like the convenience of intermittent fasting.

-It is an effective "life hack" that makes your life simpler, while improving your health at the same time. The fewer meals you need to plan for, the simpler your life will be.

-Not having to eat 3-4+ times per day (with the preparation and cleaning involved) also saves time. A lot of it.

TYPES OF INTERMITTENT FASTING:

Three methods of intermittent fasting are alternate day fasting, periodic fasting, and time-restricted feeding:

1. **Alternate day fasting**:
   involves alternating between a 24-hour "fast day" when the person eats less than 25% of usual energy needs, followed by a 24-hour non-fasting "feast day" period. It is the strictest form of intermittent fasting because there are more days of fasting per week.

   There are two subtypes:

   (a) **Complete alternate day fasting (total intermittent energy restriction):**
   where no calories are consumed on fast days.
   -Eat Stop Eat involves a 24-hour fast once or twice per week.

-By fasting from dinner one day to dinner the next day, this amounts to a full 24-hour fast.

-For example, if you finish dinner at 7 p.m. Monday and don't eat until dinner at 7 p.m. the next day, you've completed a full 24-hour fast. You can also fast from breakfast to breakfast or lunch to lunch —the end result is the same.

-Water, coffee, and other zero-calorie beverages are allowed during the fast, but no solid foods are permitted.

-If you're doing this to lose weight, it's very important that you eat normally during the eating periods. In other words, you should eat the same amount of food as if you hadn't been fasting at all.

-The potential downside of this method is that a full 24-hour fast may be fairly difficult for many people. However, you don't need to go all in right away. It's fine to start with 14–16 hours, then move upward from there.

(b) **Modified alternate-day fasting (or partial intermittent energy restriction)** which allows the consumption of up to 25% of daily calorie needs on fasting days instead of complete fasting. This is akin to alternating days with normal eating and days with a very-low-calorie diet.

-In alternate-day fasting, you fast every other day.

-There are several different versions of this method. Some of them allow about 500 calories during the fasting days.

-A full fast every other day can seem rather extreme, so it's not recommended for beginners.

-With this method, you may go to bed very hungry several times per week, which is not very pleasant and probably unsustainable in the long term.

2. Periodic fasting or whole-day fasting:

-involves any period of consecutive fasting of more than 24 hours, where there are one or two fast days per week, to the more extreme version with several days or weeks of fasting. During the fasting days, consumption of approximately 500 to 700 calories, or about 25% of regular daily caloric intake, may be allowed instead of complete fasting.

-For example, you might eat normally every day of the week except Mondays and Thursdays. For those two days, you eat 2 small meals of 250 calories each for women and 300 calories each for men

3. Time-restricted feeding:

-involves eating only during a certain number of hours each day. Skipping a meal and the 16:8 diet (16 fasting hours cycled by 8 non-fasting hours) are examples. This schedule is thought to leverage the circadian rhythm.

-intermittent fasting if a sudden shock to body but don't worry it will adjust by itself and even set back hormones.

-Preliminary evidence indicates that intermittent fasting may be effective for weight loss, may decrease insulin resistance and fasting insulin, and may improve cardiovascular and metabolic health, although the long term sustainability of these effects has not been studied.

4. WORRIERS DIET:

-It involves eating small amounts of raw fruits and vegetables during the day and eating one huge meal at night. Basically, you fast all day and feast at night within a four-hour eating window. The Warrior Diet was one of the first popular diets to include a form of intermittent fasting. This diet's food choices are quite similar to that of the paleo diet — mostly whole, unprocessed foods.

5. SPONTANEOUS MEAL SKIPPING DIET:

- It's a myth that people need to eat every few hours lest they hit starvation mode or lose muscle. Your body is well equipped to handle long periods of famine, let alone missing one or two meals from time to time. Just make sure to eat healthy foods during the other meals. Skipping one or two meals when you feel inclined to do so is basically a spontaneous intermittent fast. Thus, if you're really not hungry one day, skip breakfast and just eat a healthy lunch and dinner. Or, if you're travelling somewhere and can't find anything you want to eat, do a short fast.

-You don't need to follow a structured intermittent fasting plan to reap some of its benefits. Another option is to simply skip meals from time to time, such as when you don't feel hungry or are too busy to cook and eat.

NOTE: Intermittent fasting has not yet been studied in children, elderly, or underweight people, and can be harmful in these populations. Intermittent fasting is not recommended for people who are underweight, Heart patients, Type1 Diabetes, highly stressed people, people suffering with uric acid issue. The long- term sustainability of intermittent fasting is unknown.

-Intermittent fasting is not recommended for pregnant or breastfeeding women, female who are trying to conceive, or growing children and adolescents, or individuals vulnerable to eating disorders.

BENEFITS OF INTERMITTENT FASTING:

1.IMPROVES INSULIN SENSITIVITY: Regulates blood sugar levels

-As you are not eating carbohydrates for a long time, there is no glucose load in the body and thus insulin has no work. If insulin production is less it is good for body otherwise if it secrets more it has bad affects to body. Thus, helps in weight loss and increase healing.

2. IMPROVES THE LEVEL OF HUMAN GROWTH HORMONE INCREASES:

-In intermittent fasting the secretion of human growth hormone increases, when you are at normal diet the secretion of growth hormone is low but if you are doing intermittent fasting diet the secretion of growth hormone will be 5 times more than normal.

-Important point about growth hormone is it will secret while you are "SLEEPING",I.e. minimum 7-8 hours sound sleep is essential, otherwise you will go in stress and growth hormone will not release in its full potential.

***Role of growth hormone (GH) in our body**

a) GH is to spare protein in our body thus save muscle mass and make body fat more accessible for energy thus help burn fat really fast, starts your weight loss journey very soon.

b) Growth hormone improves muscle and bone strength.

c) Enhance your mood (cures stress and depression).

d) Improves memory and provides brain clarity.

e) Reduce the risk of cardiovascular disease.

f) Increases Basal metabolic rate (BMR)

g) works as antiaging, leads to age reversal. Actually, growth hormone secrets more in children's and young age, as age increases after 30's the secretion of growth hormone decreases. But by intermittent fasting it again increases.

h) Help cell repair, increase life span.

i) Reduce brain fog, increase alertness, improves more focus.

j) Has a great impact on Adrenal hormone.

3. INTERMITTENT FASTING INCREASES BRAIN HORMONE: It has neuroprotective effect.

-called BDNF Brain-derived neurotrophic factor (BDNF), and may aid the growth of new nerve cells. It may also protect against Alzheimer's disease.

-Contributes to neuroplasticity less contribution to dementia and Alzheimer's.

4. INTERMITTENT FASTING HELPS CELLULAR REPAIR:

-In intermittent fasting body cells initiate cellular repair process. This include autophagy, where cell digest and remove the old and worn out cells and dysfunctional protein that build up inside cells.

5. INTERMITTENT FASTING HAS AUTOPHAGY AFFECTS: A powerful detox method.

-Any overgrowth occurs in your body and you don't know e.g. tissue overgrowth in uterus, cyst, breast tumors.

-In autophagy these bad cells eat themselves which is very beneficial for the body that is best benefit of intermittent fasting.

-Autophagy means death of bad cells/ cancer cells and regulate new cells (cell regeneration) specially in conditions like Fatty liver, cancer.

- intermittent fasting help cell regeneration.

- within 6 months 25% of liver regenerates by intermittent fasting.

NOTE: In case of fatty liver it comes in diagnosis repot only when 90% of your cell becomes fatty.

6. INTERMITTENT FASTING HELPS IN CHANGE IN GENE EXPRESSION:

-There are changes in the function of gene related to longevity and protection against disease's

-Boost immunity

-speed up metabolism.

-Improves digestion.

-feel more energetic.

-Detoxification.

-Enhance mood, benefits your soul.

-keep your heart healthy.

-Hormonal balance.

7. HELPS IN HEALTHY WEIGHTS LOSS

-The main reason that intermittent fasting works for weight loss is that it helps you eat fewer calories.

-All of the different protocols involve skipping meals during the fasting periods.

-Unless you compensate by eating much more during the eating periods, you'll be consuming fewer calories.

-People also experienced a 4–7% reduction in waist circumference, indicating that they lost belly fat.

-These results indicate that intermittent fasting can be a useful weight loss tool.

-That said, the benefits of intermittent fasting go way beyond weight loss.

-It also has numerous benefits for metabolic health, and it may even help reduce the risk of cardiovascular disease.

-Although calorie counting is generally not required when doing intermittent fasting, the weight loss is mostly mediated by an overall reduction in calorie intake.

-Studies comparing intermittent fasting and continuous calorie restriction show no difference in weight loss when calories are matched between groups.

8. PREVENT HORMONAL IMBALANCE:

-The non-communicable diseases like diabetes, thyroid, PCOD, cholesterol, it has observed now all the problems have origin in hormone called "INSULIN". Insulin called fat storing hormone.

-When you are not eating for whole day and eating for only 8 hours you will get "less insulin spike". Hence, hence you will get a good balance of hormones.

-All hormonal imbalances cause due to mother hormone Insulin and intermittent fasting directly regulates your insulin hormone and also lowers your cholesterol levels.

STEPS TO INTERMITTENT FASTING

1. DURATION:

-You divide your day in two windows one is eating window and fasting window.

-The ideal window period if 16/8 window means, 16 hours fasting window and 8 hours eating window.

-For people who get hungry in the morning and like to eat breakfast, this method may be hard to get to use to at first. However, many breakfast skippers instinctively eat this way.

- You can drink water, black coffee (without milk) and other Zero-calorie beverages, during the fast, which can help reduce feeling of hunger.

-It is very important to primarily eat healthy foods during every eating window. This method won't work if you eat lots of junk foods or an excessive number of calories.

-Initially don't directly jump to 16/8 window, move gradually towards standard window, otherwise you are going to face some other problems or side effects.

NOTE: To start with any type of fasting body preparation is very important.

-Start practicing intermittent fasting with 12/12 window means 12 hour fasting window and 12 hours eating window. Slowly benefits start. If you want more benefits slowly increase your fasting window.

-Gradually increase your fasting window by 1hour per week

-Initially to start with in first week (for 1st 7 days) start with 12/12 window means 12 hours fasting and 12 hours eating window.

-In 2nd week increasing your fasting window by 1 more hour start with 13/11 window means 13 hours fasting and 11 hours eating window.

-in 3rd week go for 14/10 window, means 14 hours fasting and 10 hours eating window.

NOTE: For women wo are already in some stress in their life if they could reach this stage is also very beneficial, they start experiencing its benefits.

-4th week you can go up to 15/9 that is 15 hours fasting and 9 hours eating window.

-5th week, after a continues and gradual practice of 15 hours fasting you can finally reach to an ideal fasting window of 16/8 means 16 hours fasting and 8 hours eating window.

-6th week in addition to 16/8 window for 6 days you can go with one day detox diet (no grains only fruits and vegetable diet) in intermittent fasting.

2. TIPS TO SELECT DURATION OF FASTING TIMES:

-Weight loss fasting -do for 13 hours.

-Anti-aging fasting- do for 16 hours fasting.

-Cancer fasting- do for 18 hours.

-Select intermittent fasting day for at least 2 times/week, when you have busy seclude where you don't have much time to focus on food.

-NOTE: Intermittent fasting is not a diet plan it is a lifestyle. It is easy to fallow, once your body get used to it, you can continue it for lifelong.

3. NUMBER OF DAYS IN A WEEK:

-Initially there is no need of doing all 7 days of week.

-you can start with 12/12 for all 7 days, it will be easy for you.

- some time not for whole week but you can fallow the intermittent fasting once or twice a week, depending upon a day prior how it was like if you had heavy meals or heavy snacks, very little physical activity you can go for fasting next day.

-if you have busy seclude and stressful situation in a day, you can break your fast with guilt free and enjoy all your 3 meals but take care of portion size and nutrition of your diet which you are consuming.

-once in a week if you can do detox diet, then go ahead it is very beneficial for you, where you eat only liquids, salads (An antioxidant rich diet).

4. TIMINGS:

for example

-12-12 window start from 8am-8pm.

-13-11 window starts from 9am-8pm.

-14-10 window starts from 10am-8pm.

-15-9 window starts from 10 am -7pm.

-16-8 window starts from 11 am-7pm.

NOTE: Try and eat dinner 2-3 hour before bed time.

5. WHAT TO EAT IF YOU FEEL LOW IN FASTING WINDOW

-You can have "BULLET COFFEE"

-Recipe: Take 1 cup boiling hot water, 1tsp Butter, 1tsp coconut oil, 1 and ½ tsp of coffee grounded. blend all together and have it.

6. HOW MANY MEALS IN A DAY

FOR EXAMPLE, you can have.

-2 main meals and 2-3 small meals (snacks).

- 3 main meals and 1 snack.

-3 small meals and 1-2 snack (ideal for weight loss)

Tips for weight loss:

-Take small meals.

-Reduce portion size.

-Open fast with: preferably with light foods like fruits.

NOTE: opening fast window with heavy foods can cause stomach cramps, bloating, discomfort.

-Any digestive issues take 5 small meals.

7. WHAT TO EAT DURING EATING WINDOW

-Have natural foods: Eat fresh fruits and vegetables, green leafy vegetables.

-Have Protein: plant protein (dals, legumes and pulses), milk and milk products (milk, curd, buttermilk, paneer), Animal protein (lean protein, egg, chicken, fish).

-Have complex carbohydrates: whole grains (single polish rice, whole wheat), millets (Finger millet (ragi), sorghum (jowar), Pearl millet (bajra), foxtail millet, Sama millet), Oats, barley, quinoa.

- Have diet rich in vitamin B, C, D, E, A, K and mineral iron, calcium, potassium, zinc.

- Have diet rich in Antioxidant.

- Add apple cider vinegar to your lifestyle.

WHAT ARE THE DRAWBACKS OR UNABLE TO DO INTERMITTENT FASTING?

-Always thinking about food, they can't handle fasting.

-Overeating: we usually tend to overeat in eating window because of that we are not going to get any food.

-Eating junk: many people think of "see I have done 16hours fasting now I can eat how much I can", no it's a bad idea.

-Stress: fasting stress or other stress (physical, psychological or emotional stress)

-Sleep: Peaceful sleep is important in intermittent fasting because sleep allows body to heal and repair.

MISTAKES OF INTERMITTENT FASTING:

1.NOT EATING HEALTHY:
-You are still into eating processed, packed, outside food.

-Eat more natural, home cooked, including large amount vegetables.

2.NOT DRINKING ENOUGH FLUID:
-Increase intake of water.

-Stay hydrated.

-consume at least 35ml/kg body weight. Example: If your weight is 75kg, $35 \times 75 = 2625$ml which means a person with 75kg body weight need to consume at least 2.6 liters of fluid per day.

OTHERS DRINKS ALLOWED IN FASTING ARE:
-Plain water.

-Herbal tea.

-Green tea.

-Herbal infused water (methi or cinnamon water)

-Detox water.

-Lemon water.

-Alovera juice.

-Black coffee.

-Apple cider vinegar in water.

NOTE: Do not add honey to any of the above it increases the calorie which breaks your fast.

3.STRESS: INCEASED STRESS LEVELS
-Do intermittent only when you are stress free.

-In stress especially belly fat increases (central obesity) if you are fasting in stress.

-In stress the level of Cortisol increases which in turn increases fat levels in body, because cortisol is a fat storing hormone.

-In stress weight loss becomes very difficult.

- Stress also have various other side effects on body and brain.

4. SLEEP: Sound sleep of 6-8 hours/day is required.

-To get the complete benefits of intermittent fasting we need a good release of Human growth hormone. Which can happen only when we have a sound good quality sleep for 6-8 hours /day.

-Human growth hormone releases in sleep.

5. IMPROPER EATING PATTERNS: OVEREATING/UNDEREATING

-We try to fit full day diet plan/ Try to fit many meals in your diet plan, in your eating window.

-Either eat whenever you are hungry or prepare a fixed seclude.

-Taking a very low-calorie diet can slow down your metabolism and leads to fat accumulation, resulting in weight gain.

6. NOT EATING HEALTHY FAT.

-One should eat 1-3 tsp of visible fat on daily basis.

-Example like desi cow ghee, coconut oil, mustard oil, olive oil, flax seeds, chia seeds, almonds, walnut are good source and have omega 3 which is very healthy in moderation.

7. HAVING TOO MUCH CAFFEINE

-Limit your consumption of caffeine.

-Don't drink caffeinated drink with and immediately after meal.

-Avoid caffein empty stomach and post sunset.

-Average dose of consumption 1-2 serving per day.

8. NOT MATCHING WINDOW (FASTING/EATING) WITH ACTIVITY LEVEL.

-Keep your workout seclude, either close to or within the eating window.

-choose a window that matches your activity level.

-Eat when you are most active and fast when you are less active.

-Alternate the window timings to match your routine.

9. NOT CHOOSING RIGHT PLAN

-Other way of doing intermittent fasting. should be done very carefully, do not overdo it otherwise it can show its side effects and there can be also a chance of losing lean muscle mass.

-5:2 fasting (allows only 500calories twice a week), not more than that.

-24 hours complete fasting once a week.

-12/12 hours fasting for beginners.

NOTE: Eat lots of vegetables, at least 2 servings per day. And eat fruits at least 1 serving per day. In intermittent fasting.

10. **DON'T BE OBSESSED WITH CLOCK.**

-Constant watching clock for time that when my eating window will start and when can I have my meal, it will build lot of **stress and you won't get the benefits of** intermittent fasting.

NOTE: Don't go for 16:8 window directly, start with 12:12 window gradually increase 1 hour for every one week, slowly adjust your body.

SIDE EFFECTS OF INTERMITTENT FASTING

1. **Missing Nutrition:**

-You are missing one whole meal to take of this do include "Dark green leafy" in your meal it will help to add lots of vitamins and minerals to you diet to cove the missing nutritional deficiency.

-In case if you are non-vegetarian you can add a piece of liver (organ meat) to your non veg curry (chicken/mutton) it adds lot of nutrition to your meal.

-You may develop allergies if you are nutrient deficient it can show its side effects on your skin, hair & nails.

2. **Affects your digestive system:**

-Because it is not ready to take so much of food load at once.

-If you break your fast with heavy meals and lots of proteins it could be possible that you can have crashes.

-To prevent this side effect do not open your fast with heavy meals.

3. **No weight lifting when you are in intermittent fasting window**

-strength training on your own body weight is ok but do not go for weight lifting, dead lift it can cause sever loss in lean muscle mass.

- It can also compromise your bone mineral density.

Q) How to get maximum benefits of Intermittent fasting for weight loss?

-Drink "Apple cider vinegar" in fasting it helps to mobilize the fat and when you don't eat anything then it starts eating your body's stored fat.

-Physical activity: when you are about to break your fast like you had your dinner at 9pm and you will have your breakfast at 1pm, which shows 16 hours fasting. Before breaking your fast do 20 min off sprints it will have added benefits, you can also do high intensity interval training (HIIT) and eat your meals.

Q) Can working out during fasting window period leads to muscle loss?

-Exercise in fasting utilize glycogen tank stored fat from body helps in weight loss. And ultimately leads to fat loss.

-If we do weight training, we should eat (open fast) immediately after exercise, its means you need to break your fast immediately after exercise.

-If strength training (on your own body weight) or regular exercise (yoga, stretches, walking, lite jogging) for 30-45 minutes in a day. if there is 2-3 hours gap in opening fast there is no problem.

-Research shows that to start eating window (breaking fast) after workout it is not for 2 hours or half an hour it stays open for almost 3-4 hours, if you want to repair your muscles you can do it. it is not compulsory that just now you have completed your workout and immediately you rush and eat something. That happens only when you're doing weight training by using lots of weights, usually after any type of workout the contraction and relaxation of muscle occur this process continuous after that you can have your food. It will use that stored fat it will not cause any muscle loss.

Q) what if growling sounds coming from your stomach during fasting window?

-Initially your body sends all signals that you should eat, that is perfectly normal, if growling sounds is coming means your body is just sending the signals where is the food use it.

-but if your brain is low on energy you can take bulletproof coffee (300kcal) but don't make habit of it and don't over-do it. Just take a support in initial stage of fasting period.

Q) IS SKIPPING BREAKFAST IN INTERMITTENT FASTING HEALTHY?

- Usually we have a concept that we need to eat something as soon as we wake up and do our breakfast on time is important for our health but now when it comes to intermittent fasting, we are skipping these meals and have a question that do is really healthy to skip breakfast.

-BREAKFAST means breaking FAST, you can break your fast on your choice it can be 9am or 11 am, as you start eating food is the time of breaking your fast. You can break your fast during your secluded eating window.

-Ghrelin is a hunger hormone.

-It is high in morning at 7:30 am-8:00am in between that time if you drink a fat cutter drink (water-1liter, pinch pink Himalayan salt, pinch cinnamon powder) then this window goes away. Even diabetic patient can do this.
NOTE: The who take less salt have more heart issues.

-And from 8:00am- 11:30am the ghrelin will be low (feel no hungry).

-And again, it will be high between 12:00noon-1:00pm if we can cross that window, you can be hungry till 2:00pm.

-But they who cannot cross no issues what you need to do this.
*complete your dinner by 8pm and do your breakfast at 12:00noon-1:00pm it completes your ideal 16/8 window (16 hours fasting).
*Initially you can start 12 hours-16 hours fasting.
NOTE:
-Fasting is not so recommended for people who are already suffering from metabolic issues.
-When you are in heavy seclude or in stress do not do fsting because fasting is also stress to your body and exercise is also stress to your body during this phase .

SAMPLE DIET PLAN (An idea how to add breakfast into eating window):

11am - Break my fast with a fruit banana
11 :35 am – Breakfast Oats, eggs, vegetables
2 pm – 2nd serving of fruit (an orange or guava) in season
3 pm –lunch slightly light (dal, sabzi, one roti/1/2 cup rice with curd)
4:30 pm – Indian tea with handful of peanuts
6:30 pm –Dinner large serving of vegetables (steamed or sautéed), 2 Roti, sabzi
with gravy (paneer, tofu, beans)
6:50 pm – warm milk with masala
Note: Eat lots of vegetables and fruits, focus on eating healthy foods, keep a
check on your fluid intake, avoid consuming caffeine. By following this pattern
of eating calories will cut down automatically.

INTERMITTENT FASTING GUIDELINES FOR BIGGNERS

-Initially to start with intermittent fasting every one face many complains like

-Headache, hair loss, no weight loss, low energy or energy crash (after opening
fast), unable to stay without morning tea.

-Intermittent fasting has become famous because, our ghrelin hormone (hunger
hormone) is very low in the morning till 11am, it is very easy to miss food at this
time.

-But you have made it so habit to your body i.e. body is I search of energy.

-in this fasting window will train the body to take the energy from the body's stored
fat.

HEALTH COMPLAINS AND THEIR SOLUTIONS DURING

INTERMITTENT FASTING 1.LOW ENERGY LEVELS:

- FEEL EXCESS HUNGER:

-Many people feel that we can skip dinner in intermittent fasting, no possibly try to
skip breakfast because the hunger hormone-ghrelin will be low and it would be easy
to miss breakfast and intermittent fasting is made easy.

- We feel strong hunger pranks in the morning time, it's quite normal because your
body is habituated of eating, definitely you will feel hungry.

-we have made this habit of eating to our body now it is in our hand what how to come out of this habit. Skip this habit for 15-20 days slowly you overcome this hunger pranks. And you can easily skip your breakfast.

-1st we need to understand thar how to do intermittent fasting. E.g. if you had your dinner at 8 pm try to eat low carbohydrate dinner, and you are feeling hungry at 11pm no need to worry just drink only water.

-Next day in the morning when during your regular breakfast time in fasting window the ghrelin (hunger hormone) will raise, and you also experience groaning sounds in stomach, then you need to drink only water by adding pinch of pink Himalayan salt. Sometimes by this also your energy levels can be normal because when we are not eating anything your insulin levels will be low, insulin helps to hold the sodium and potassium levels in body, but when insulin levels become low kidneys cannot hold sodium and potassium it will excrete it out, as sodium goes out body loses its electrolytes and when you go for urine you feel low energy.

a) 1st hack: Take 1-liter water add ½ tsp of pink Himalayan salt to it and consume in your fasting window, drink lot of water, as you are not eating anything your insulin will come down, insulin helps to hold water in body and kidney.

NOTE: But that doesn't mean that you should drink 4-5 liters of water/day it will dilute the electrolytes like magnesium, sodium, potassium, extracts through urine. Due to loss of electrolytes you will feel low energy.

b) 2nd hack: Take caffeine it will give you energy. (caffeine is appetite suppressant)

-1cup of black tea = 50mg caffeine.

-1 cup of coffee = 100 mg caffeine.

-1 cup of green tea = 30mg caffeine.

NOTE: Due to its caffeine levels, initially start with green tea if energy levels are not recovered next go to black tea and if not, finally you can have black coffee. but do not overdo coffee because it will deplete vitamin B and magnesium levels from body.

c) 3rd hack: initially first 21days of intermittent fasting when you open your fast make sure you need to take magnesium and vitamin B supplement. It will sustain your good energy levels and prevent form low energy levels.

d) 4th hack: for constant hunger in stomach, hunger won't go away

-Take bullet coffee (boiling water 1 cup+ butter 1tsp+ coconut oil 1tsp blend).

-And you can take supplements with it like ADK, omega 3, B vitamin.

e) 5th hack: Take proper meal (specially protein) during your eating window.

-Complains like hair fall, dark circles, nails break this all cause due to protein deficiency.

-What is food -It carries food information

e.g. spinach- iron- good for brain strength.

Paneer- protein- good for your skin and hair.

2. HEADACHE DURING FASTING PERIOD

-You feel like headache because your brain is expecting that you are going to get carbohydrates, which are used as energy to brain and body, when your brain do not get energy it will feel low, in that case you can have 1 tsp coconut oil or you can have bullet coffee as soon as you stomach start showing groaning sounds.

-by this simple issue don't say that I am going to give up intermittent fasting I cannot do it, slowly make a habit of it by giving simple tasks to body. Your body slowly get used to it by in morning times not eating food and survive only on fat.

3. DARKCIRCLES AND HAIRFALL:

-It is bound to happen because fasting is stress to your body, and weight loss is also stress to your body already our environmental toxic load is high and our bodies nutrition value is not fulfilled on top of that we have taken away one more meal from our daily diet then the result is nutrition deficiency.

-If the body is nutrient deficient then hair says I am deficient with nutrients and our body's vital organs like lungs, kidney, heart, brain, which are important for our survival need to focus on them, and they neglect hair, nails and skin becomes secondary to body and thus your body shed hair, nails , skin becomes dry, dark circles undereye. What you need to do in this point is need to increase your nutrition levels. e.g. when you are opening your fast take highly nutritious food like mixed green leafy saag, green smoothie, etc.

-You also need to take supplement's like iron tablets because if you have hair fall that means you have less blood circulation and you need to improve your iron levels.

-Take B12, Proteins (you can mix whey and collagen protein mix) make a protein shake and open your fast with it or integrate it in your eating window.

4. NO WEIGHT LOSS:

-Many people say being doing intermittent fasting I am unable to do weight loss.

-weight loss happens when you go calorie deficient.

-It doesn't mean, if you are fasting you have right to eat anything you wish. e.g. we skip breakfast to go in calorie deficient like 300-350kcal is removed and during your eating window if you eat 1 muffin which is about 250-300kcal, then there will be no weight loss. you need to go calorie deficient.

-Special focus is needed on protein because it has thermogenic effect, because to digest protein it requires 20% of calories.

5. WEIGHT STAGNANT:

-For that you need to take your body to next level.

Trick 1: INCREASE YOUR ACTIVITY LEVEL.

-20-25 minutes workout.

-You are not eating anything from morning do some simple workout even walking is ok no need of doing high intensity.

-Research shows "fat metabolization and fat oxidation increases during intermittent fasting while moving".

-If you want to do high intensity it will lead to more weight loss, your body is in search of energy as you don't provide energy from food then your body will start taking energy from your body's stored fat cells but immediately you need to open your fast otherwise it causes muscle loss.

-And also, be aware of calories in feeding window by eating lots of veggies and lean protein e.g. pea, chicken, curd.

-Try and see once in a day OMAD (one meal in a day)

NOTE: specially for women as they need more nutrition for their hormones, do not force yourself for OMAD, slowly make a habit of it, once your body is ready you can go for it, and after that you need to provide nutritional supplements to your body.

6. ENERGY CRASH:

-Energy crash occurs immediately after opening the fast, because due to fast your body becomes insulin sensitive, your body won't expect carbohydrates, proteins and fats in your blood and on top your digestive enzymes are settled down.

-If you give heavy meals where your body is not ready for it because blood from your brain get diverted to digestive system and thus brain gets crash.

-Before opening your fast have apple cider vinegar, due to fasting your stomach acid has gone down by taking apple cider vinegar you get support of acid.

-you can also take Alovera juice, amla juice. Or you can open your fast with a fruit e.g. watermelon, apple, any seasonal fruit. Your body becomes ready for further main meal.

- Have a small meal after taking apple cider vinegar like (curd with seeds like chia seeds, flax seeds and next go for main meal specially include only lean protein no high carbohydrates and high fats meals. After this also you feel energy crash then it means your body is resistant that your body cannot handle glucose. For them there is high chance of getting diabetes.

-After this also if you feel crash take mineral chromium (1000mcg) it handles insulin very well which help carbohydrates to enter from blood to your cells so that energy which is produced is not loosed.

Intermittent fasting MEN Vs WOMEN?

- For women fasting could be stress for the body, as hormones in women changes continuously, fasting in this condition for women can build up more stress and can also lead for hormonal imbalance.

-Women should not start intermittent fasting for full week, just start intermittent fasting with once a week and slowly gain momentum to twice a week and then on you can do intermittent fasting in every alternate day.

-In case of Men fasting is not so stressful condition unless they have stress belly, men can adopt fasting as everyday lifestyle.

-Male and female body react in different way during fasting period. Pattern of eating is based on that reaction.

-It is more beneficial for males then females. For females to follow successful intermittent fasting they need to follow the following points:

1) Why intermittent fasting has different effect on female body?

As compared to men women have different

- Reproductive system
- Menstrual cycle
- Genetic make up
- Female hormones
- Neurological makeup

Hence it is very important to modify the standard intermittent fasting pattern to match with the need of female

2) Possible side effects of intermittent fasting on female body

As follows

- Low energy
- Mood swings
- Low concentration
- Headache
- Sleep issues
- Disturbance in period cycle
- Hair loss
- Loose skin

- Muscle loss
- Feeling cold

3) Possible reasons for side effects on female

As follows

- Low calories diet combined with intermittent fasting
- Low carbs or other fad diets
- Poor nutrition
- Long fasting hours
- Nutritional deficiencies
- High levels of stress
- Wrong workout at wrong time
- Hormonal imbalance
- Unhealthy life style
- Disrupt the release of reproductive hormones like utilizing hormone and follicle stimulating hormone
- Effects the level of estrogen
- Release more leptin
- All this can have effect on metabolism, periods, bones, hair and skin

4) Why does all these changes happen while a female is fasting

- Fasting stage starts when body start using stored fat for energy i.e., this happens when the energy from last meal is exhausted by our body.
- Then for energy the fat stored in our body is utilized. This is a good sign for weight loss and fat loss.
- But female bodies do not like this. Most of the female bodies like to store fat in their body. This is because whenever the body requires to use the stored fat most of the female bodies react negatively, body releases more leptin, energy level decreases, metabolism decreases. So, in general female body does not like fasting to a great extent.

5) Solution for female who face above mentioned problem in intermittent fasting

Types of intermittent fasting

- Standard 16:8 method (Lean gain method)
- Time restricted method i.e., <u>**CRESCENDO FASTING**</u> **12:12 (simple fasting), 13:11, 14:10 (Brunch fasting)**
- 5:2 method
- OMAD
- Warrior Diet

CRESCENDO FASTING works amazing for females

- In this method there are 3 stages 12:12 window i.e., 12 hours eating and 12 hours fasting this is called simple fasting
- 13:11 window & 14:10 window are known as Brunch fasting i.e., we break fast late in the morning. This is the safest window for females. Once or twice a week we can take a break from intermittent fasting and follow regular diet/any detox diet to take full advantage, which is good for females. It is stress relieving.
- My advice is to go with Crescendo fasting if you are trying intermittent fasting

6) Intermittent fasting tips for women

As Follows

- Follow crescendo fasting
- Dink cinnamon, rock salt water in fasting window
- Eat nutritious dense diet
- Stay hydrated
- Eat Lean protein
- Eat healthy fat in moderation
- Avoid stress
- Workout close to or in feeding window
- Take 1-2 off days in a week
- Weekly detox
- Take proper rest
- Stop counting calories
- Have nutritious food
- Add omega-3 fatty acid food like Almons, Chia seeds etc.

INTERMITTENT FASTING COMPLET GUIDE FOR WOMEN

Q) WHAT ARE THE SIDE EFFECT SYMPTOMS OF INTERMITTENT FASTING ON WOMEN BODY IF THEY ARE NOT DOING IT PROPERLY?

The symptoms are as follows

-They miss their periods.

-Hormonal imbalance.

-Permanent change in gut bacteria.

-weight gets stuck.

-Adrenal fatigue (tired body).

-Worst mood swings.

-Anxiety.

-Skin gets affected.

-Disturbed sleep.

- Hair is affected because of lack of resources.

1. HOW TO DO CORRECT INTERMITTENT FASTING FOR WOMEN:

-If you want to burn fat and gain maximum benefits do fat fast.

-***If you are suffering from any of this issue** like Thyroid, Hormonal imbalance, Irregular periods, Uric acid issues, Fatigue, Anxiety, Insomnia, dark circles.

-solution for this is you need to do "Fat Fast" because hormones are made out of fat.

a) FAT FAST:

-Tea (coconut milk)

-Coffee (1tsp extra virgin coconut oil+1tsp butter) blend.

-If your gallbladder is removed take fat tea/coffee + digestive enzyme.

-or simple take 1 tsp of extra virgin coconut oil.

BENEFITS IF FAT FAST:

-Kills craving.

-Autophagy do not occur.

-No detoxification but weight loss will be there.

-Neuroprotective affects in brain is developed.

***The who do workout in empty stomach (i.e. in fasting window)**

-If we exercise on empty stomach there will be muscle loss and for the women whose skin in getting loose with fasting, dark circles, hair fall.

-They need to focus on quality protein. specially BCAA (Branch chain ammino acid) unflavored, unsweetened.

2. HOW TO DO MAXIMUM FAT BURN IN INTERMITTET FASTING

- Studies shows in women muscle fiber it contains more of fat as compared to men

- which means during fasting if we even move a little as compared to men, the availability of fat for weight loss and for energy is more. You will experience more fat loss as compared to men.

- Right movements which help you for fat loss during intermittent fasting: walk, household works, climbing staircase, yoga, palates, next level is HIIT (High intensity interval training)

NOTE: the only hack is immediately after HIIT you need to open your fast.

3. HOW TO USE FASTING AS ANTI AGING TOOL?

- As we cross Thirty years, we develop fine lines, wrinkles etc. we age because our cells are aging.
- Our DNA in cells have chromosomes with talomeial length. Which is formed by eating fat. With age the talomeial length shortens and they either die or become ageing.
- Whenever we do intermittent fasting, we should at least do it for 16 hours
- In this when you break your fast do keto diet (low in carbohydrates and high in fat, lean protein). It is the most powerful anti-aging hack.

PHASES OF INTERMITTENT FASTING & Its BENEFITS:

i)   **Phase I: Startup 12 hours fasting** – 8 pm dinner to 8 am breakfast. **Benefits:** Craving for full day will be less, weight loss will be light, reduce leptin resistance.

ii)   **Phase II: 16 hours fasting, 8 hours eating** (at least three times per week) **Benefits:** Powerful benefit autophagy (detoxification), cognition clarity, diabetic regulation, reset gut bacteria.

iii)   **Phase III: Along with 16/8 hours fasting start with OMAD** (one meal in a day) **once a week.** **Benefits:** regenerate new cells, reduce digestion issues, improves mucosal layer, reduce inflammations in body.

iv)   **Phase IV: Full day fast (once in a month).** You can drink water **Note:** Here take care of nutrition and supplements to prevent nutritional deficiencies.

PROLONG FASTING:

HOW TO DO PROLONG FASTING: -

-Start with intermittent fasting and slowly go for karvachot fasting i.e., drinking only water and not eating the whole day.

-Start your day with one glass water by adding $1/4^{th}$ teaspoon of pink Himalayan salt as insulin goes down due to fasting. The insulin hold sodium in body which in turn holds water in body. As insulin goes down body's kidney will lead to frequent urination and your sodium levels goes down. You will feel low energy.

WHEN TO DO PROLONG FASTING: AND ITS BENEFITS.

i)   Weight gets stuck or

ii)   If you want extra detox(autophagy), if you don't eat for 24 – 48 hours it stimulates your immune system.

iii)   It will reset your digestive system ex: farting, brain fog after food, that means you have digestive issue, gas issue.

iv)   In fasting our mucosal lining regenerates do not require antiacid.

v) Women cheapest antiaging hack, because women body is more capable of mobilising and metabolising fat in body compared to men.

vi) Fasting help to increase length of telemores of DNA and our hair, skin cell won't die soon.

vii) Stem cell regeneration increases.

GENERAL MISTAKES COMMITED BY MANY PEOPLE DURING INTERMITTENT FASTING:

1. MOVING FAST TO ACHIVE QUICK RESULTS:

-If you try to move too fast, you may feel overburden is given to body because sudden change to body initially body won't accept it and feel discomfort when for sudden you stop giving food to body for certain time.

-For that we need to slowly move towards standard window of 16/8 (16hours fasting and 8 hours eating) always listen to your body before starting your window, you need to be aware of the changes in your body.

-If you feeling light headache, fatigue, low on energy that means you have not chosen the right window maybe you need to go slow, gradually move towards your 16/8 window, for women 16/8 is not must 14/10 is also enough.

2. NOT INCLUDING HIGH FIBER FOOD IN YOUR DIET:

-It is very important to include fruits, vegetables, whole grains, nuts, seeds, pulses and legumes In your eating window, eat real and unprocessed food. You feel satisfied for long period of time.

-If there is lot of consumption of refined food it will be not only unhealthy to your body but also you may feel more fatigue.

-Soluble fibre is very beneficial if you are doing intermittent fasting. This type of fibre dissolves in water to form a gel-like material. It can help lower blood cholesterol and glucose levels. Soluble fibre is found in oats, peas, beans, apples. Citrus fruits, carrots, barley and psyllium husk, etc.

3. AVOID INTENSE WORKOUT IN FASTING WINDOW:

-You can only do if your workout is lite and less intense like yoga, stretches, walking and lite jogging is fine.

-To do intense workout make sure that it could be close to your eating window or it is in your eating window.

-If you over train your body and you do not feed it can cause loss of muscle mass, it will drop your metabolism and immunity, it may show lot of negative effects on your body.

-According to the research that doing exercise daily will increase life span of an individual. In this they have shown that doing exercise shows positive impact on your body (increase your life span) and not doing any physical activity shows negative impact (decrease your life span) but if we overtrain or overdo exercise then it will definitely shows negative impact on body (your life span will decrease more) which lead to symptoms like mood swings, loss of appetite, frequent cold and infection, elevated morning heart rate, muscle soreness, persistent fatigue, struggling with training and performance, lack of focus, sleep issues.

4. NOT CHOOSING THE RIGHT WINDOW:

-It is not about the timing but about the window your choosing, every individual has his own prime time only thing you need to choose right.

-For example, few people feel eating breakfast is very important for them keep your eating window in the morning, for few dinners is important keep window to dinner time, only make sure keep in mind about your activity levels only choose your eating window.

-Choosing the right window is equally important than fasting.

5. NUMBER OF MEALS AND THEIR PORTION SIZE:

-If you are eating same number of meals then you need to cut down the portion size of your meal.

-If you don't cut down your portion size you will feel bloated and do not overfeed yourself.

6. NOT EATING ENOUGH FOOD/CALORIES:

-Many people try to choose different fad diets during intermittent fasting eating window like low calorie diet, low carb diet and many more in which diet is very much deficient in calories. here you are eating for less duration and less in calories.

-If you are deficient in your maintenance calories for long duration then your metabolic rate, immunity and muscle mass goes more down. That's why make sure you are taking enough calories.

-Average daily calorie requirement: For healthy adult women is 1300-1800kcal, and for Men is 1800-2200kcal.

-If you are willing for weight loss you can cut down 200-250 kcal per day not more than that otherwise it shows negative impact on body.

7. INTERMITTENT FASTING IS NOT FOR EVERYONE:

-Intermittent fasting is one of the healthiest ways to lose weight but it is not the same for everyone like. E.g. if you are less then 18 years old or if you are above 70 years.

-similarly, if you are on any medication where you need to take medicine 3 times a day on a specific time or on empty stomach then consult your doctor to know how to manage it. If you are diabetic then also you need to consult your doctor then after you can do it.

8. NOT DRINKING ENOUGH WATER/NOT STAYING HYDERATED:

-Drinking enough water in fasting period is very important.

-you can also consume some other drinks during your fasting window like detox water, any healthy drink under 20 kcal. Do not add chia seeds to your detox water it will increase its calorific value more than 20kcal.

-If you want to consume bullet tea or coffee it depends upon your goals like – going for fat loss is not healthy,

-Consuming Bullet tea or coffee is not healthy for people who go for fat loss but it is healthy for people whose goal is muscle gain or for general health.

9. TOO MUCH CAFFEINE (TEA/COFFEE):

-Green tea or black coffee is allowed in fasting window. But over consumption of effects their health. Too much of anything is bad

- Two cups of Green tea in a day is good but consuming more than that shows negative impact of health because Caffeine content in green tea immediately stimulates your brain cells and immediately causes energy crash and nerve stimulator in excess is not good.

10. STILL FOLLOWING A POOR LIFE STYLE:

-Even while doing intermittent fasting having poor life style is not good for your health like- poor sleeping habits, unable to manage stress, over usage of gadgets, do not be over strict on body etc.

-So, maintaining a good life style, being relaxed, happy mood, stress free etc while following intermittent fasting gives good results.

11. NOT EATING HEALTHY:

-You are still into eating processed, packed, outside food.

-Eat more natural, home cooked foods, including large amount of vegetables.

BEGINNERS TIPS FOR INTERMITTENT FATSING:

- Choose a time that suits your life style
- Look at it as time restricted eating, not fasting
- Go gradually for great success (eat 3 proper meals)
- Drink lots of water
- Eat more fruits & salads
- But don't just eat lite salads
- Eat healthy & exercise
- Eat more of low glycaemic foods
- Don't drink lots of caffeine (specially in fasting period)
- Arm yourself with knowledge
- Look for suitability, consult your physician

WHO SHOULD AVOID IMF?

- People who take medications for blood pressure or heart disease
- Pregnant & breastfeeding mother's
- People with eating disorder
- People with gallstone disease
- People suffering from depression
- Women who are anaemic

- Consult a physician in case of hormonal imbalance
- Consult your doctor if you have thyroid issue
- People who suffer from hypoglycaemia and diabetics
- Not for teenage boys and girls

LESSONS LEARNED DURING INTERMITTENT FASTING:

- Try to put your fasting window as per your lifestyle because intermittent fasting is not a shortcut to lose your weight, it can be or I would say must be adopted as a lifestyle. Your body will adopt to intermittent fasting
- In intermittent fasting you loose weight as you consume less calories, but u still need to eat and drink healthy, eat lots of fresh vegetables, fruits and exercise
- Effect of fasting is different based on gender, age, stress levels and hormones
- Open your fast with light foods and close your eating window with a meal that is high in fibre, good carbs, high in protein and moderate amount of healthy fat which can keep you sustain during your fasting window and keep a proper balance in your hormones
- Intermittent fasting simplifies your life. It Can improve your discipline, focus and productivity, it may happen otherwise if you are only thinking about food and time
- Do not combine low calorie diet with intermittent fasting. It's a deadly combination. Its slow downs your metabolism, your weight may rebound.

DIET PLAN FOR INTERMITTENT FASTING

CALORIE ALLOWANCE PER DAY
Male: 2000kcal/day.
Female: 1600kcal/day.

1. **Balanced diet**: includes complex carbohydrates 55%, high quality protein 30%, healthy fat 15%.
2. **High protein diet**: includes complex carbohydrates 35%, high quality protein 50%, healthy fat 15%.
3. **Keto diet**: includes healthy fat 70%, high quality protein 25%, complex carbohydrates 5%.
4. **Balanced diet for weight loss**: includes vegetables (all seasonal and green leafy vegetables) 50%, complex carbohydrates 25%, high quality protein 25% and additional visible fat 5-10 %.

You should have a balanced diet, for example a cycle of 11am-7pm.
1. Break your fast: 11am.
a) with one serving of fresh seasonal fruits (80-100 kcal)
Example:
- Apple: 2extra small - 105kcal.
-Banana: 1 medium -101kcal.
-Cantaloupe: 2cup diced -106 kcal.
-Dates: 1 and half whole -100kcal.
-Grapes: 30 pieces -101Kcal.
-Mosambi: 1 ¼ whole -95kcal.
-Mango: 1cup sliced -107kcal.
-Orange: 2small -90kcal.
-Papaya: 2cup cubed -109kcal.
-Pear: 1medium -96kcal.
-Pineapple: 1 1/4cup -103kcal.
-Pomegranate: 1/2cup -117kcal

b) Best drink to open your fast is

- plain fresh coconut water.

-vegetable smoothie (green smoothie, beetroot or carrot smoothie blended in plane water or coconut water)

-You can have single fruit (orange juice) or vegetable juice (bottle guard juice).

-Apple cider vinegar with honey.

- super greens: spirulina, wheat grass, barley grass juice.

-if you are non-vegetarian you can open your fast with any broth e.g. chicken broth.

c)If you want to eat directly something without any drinks then you can have "soaked nuts and seeds". but be aware of portion size.

-Almonds (6-8)

-walnuts. (1 whole)

-Resins (black with seeds or golden resins) (8-10)

-Fig (1 whole)

-Dates (1-2)

-Chia seeds or basil seeds.

-Flax seeds. (flax seed water)

-Pumpkin seeds. (1tbsp)

-Sunflower seeds. (1tbsp)

-Watermelon or muskmelon seeds. (1tbsp)

These all are rich in fiber, vitamins and minerals and moderate amount of natural sugars. Do feel that eating carb during intermittent fasting is a sin, don't go for fad diets.

d) You can have steamed vegetable salad. Do not eat raw vegetable salad or drink raw vegetable juice while opening your fast. Slightly cook them and consume. because raw vegetable is hard on digestion.

NOTE: Do not break your fast by taking heavy meal or cooked grains it will create lot of load on digestive system, start with lite food on digestion like fruits or vegetables.

2. FIRST MEAL OF THE DAY -11:30am Breakfast (300-350kcal)
-You need to choose low carbohydrate diet, replace your regular food ingredients with low carbohydrate ingredients.
-If you use low carbohydrate flour You can easily eat roti e.g. by replacing wheat flour with almond flour or coconut flour. You can prepare same recipes with different low carbohydrate ingredients.
-Some time what happens after a long fast if you eat suddenly you feel fatigue because it slows down your digestion.
-So, we need to plan in such a way that as soon as we start eating the food it should not be hard on your digestive system and it should be tasty to eat and you should enjoy eating it.
-Planned recipes should give you all the required nutrients required for the proper maintenance of the body.
-Complex carbohydrates e.g. Poha, upma, quick oats, homemade granola with coconut milk, brown rice/roti (40gm) roti made out of gluten free flour like almond flour, Bengal gram flour, oats flour, coconut flour, millets like sorghum, pearl millet and finger millet flour. Try to avoid wheat flour if you have gluten allergy.
-fiber, vitamin and mineral rich: add lots of seasonal vegetables.
-fermented foods: (idly, dhokla, dosa)

-Quality protein e.g. lentil/beans/chickpea/sprouts/paneer/tofu/egg/chicken/fish +curd/buttermilk.

-Healthy fat :1 tsp ghee.

NOTE: Avoid refined, processed, packed, junk, sugary foods.

3. HAVE A LARGE SERVING OF VEGETABLES- 1:30 PM (60-80Kcal)

-e.g. Raw/semi-cooked/ steamed vegetable salad do not add any cream or nuts dressing to the salad.

-salad should be low in calorie and high in fiber, vitamins and minerals.

-Vegetable options: Brussels sprouts, broccoli, cabbage, celery, cauliflower, bell pepper, cucumber, eggplant, pumpkin, squash, tomatoes, corn, beetroot, carrot, coriander, green peas, mushroom, spinach, micro-greens, any seasonal and locally available vegetables of your choice.

4. SECOND MEAL OF THE DAY-3:30PM

-HAVE SOMETHING LITE FOOD FOR AN ABOUT 200-250KCAL.

-Example: poha(1cup) /upma(1cup)/ idly(2)/ dosa(2small)/ thepla(1 medium)/ sprouts (1cup)/ dhokla (2 slices)/ handful nuts/ panjiree (2tbsp). or any staple food of your choice, but be aware of the portion size.

5. SNACK TIME: 4pm-4:45pm (80-200kcal)

-1cup green tea/herbal tea.

-handful roasted Chana/ peanuts/ makhana/ energy bars/ protein bars/ pumpkin seeds/ sunflower seeds/ roasted seeds trial mix.

-If you are planning for any physical activity /workout in this time you can have like yoga, walk, HIIT training any of your choice.

-Pre-workout meal: any fruit/ nuts.

-Post-workout meal: any protein shake. (helps to repair and rebuild your lean muscle mass)

6. LAST MEAL OF THE DAY: 6:40 pm-7pm (300-350kcal)

 -Complex carbohydrate- wheat/barley/oats daliya, roti, mung dal kichadi.

-High quality protein- Sautee/ Grilled paneer, Tofu, mushroom, fish, 2egg whites, chicken breast, legumes/pulses.

-Add 1 cup of Sautee vegetables of your choice to your meal to increase antioxidants, fiber, vitamins and minerals.

-"EAT SLOWELY CHEW PROPERLY" for at most 20 minutes.

7. YOUR FASTING WINDOW START FROM HERE AFTER YOUR LAST MEAL.

-Do not eat or drink anything which is more than 20 kcal, because it will break your fast

-your fasting window will be continuing from 7pm till 11am next day.

-you can drink water in your fasting window.

-You can drink Fat burner drink like take 1 lit water add 1 full lemon juice, ½ tsp cinnamon powder and pinch pink Himalayan salt. Mix all well and drink sip by sip during your fasting window in the morning.